SCIENCE FACTORY

CHEMICALS
& REACTIONS

JON RICHARDS

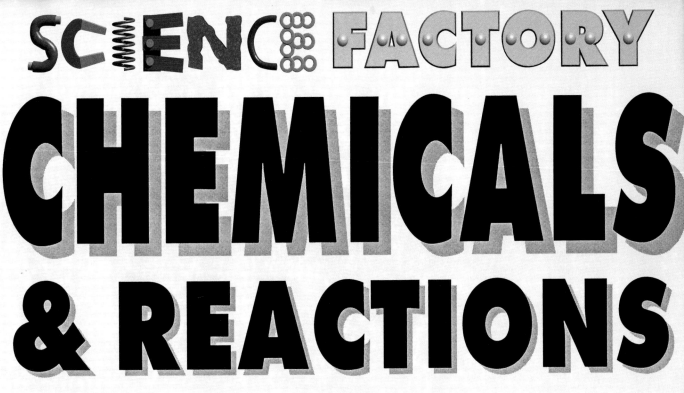

FRANKLIN WATTS
LONDON • SYDNEY

© Aladdin Books Ltd 2000

Designed and produced by
Aladdin Books Ltd
28 Percy Street
London W1P 0LD

ISBN 0 7496 3412 X

First published in Great Britain
in 2000 by
Franklin Watts Books
96 Leonard Street
London EC2A 4XD

Editor
Kathy Gemmell

Design

David West
Children's Book Design

Designer
Jennifer Skelly

Illustrator
Ian Moores

Printed in Belgium

A CIP catalogue entry for this book is
available from the British Library.

The author, Jon Richards, has written
a number of science and technology
books for children.

The consultant, Steve Parker, has
worked on over 150 books for
children, mainly on a science theme.

All the photos in this book were
taken by Roger Vlitos.

INTRODUCTION

This book looks at the basic
aspects of everyday chemistry.
Different chemical reactions
are happening all around us
all the time. When ice melts or
the kettle boils, a chemical
reaction is taking place as
water changes from solid to
liquid, or liquid to gas. By
following the projects, you can
develop your practical skills at
the same time as expanding
your scientific knowledge.

CONTENTS

YOUR FACTORY

BEFORE YOU START any of the projects, it is important that you learn a few simple rules about the care of your science factory.

● Always keep your hands and the work surfaces clean. Dirt can damage results and ruin a project.

● Read the instructions carefully before you start each project.

● Make sure you have all the equipment you need for the project (see checklist opposite).

● If you haven't got the right piece of equipment, then improvise. For example, a washing-up liquid bottle will often do just as well as a plastic drinks bottle.

● Don't be afraid to make mistakes. Just start again – patience is very important.

Equipment checklist:
- ● Plastic drinks bottles, large bowl
- ● Permanent felt-tip marker
- ● Salt, fine sand and soil
- ● Measuring jug, clingfilm, board
- ● Drinking glasses, jars, tall jar, kitchen knife
- ● Newspaper, paper, blotting paper, filter paper
- ● Flour, wholemeal flour, butter, oil, baking powder
- ● Dried yeast, caster sugar, lemon, vinegar, baking tray

- ● Red cabbage, fresh milk, washing soda
- ● Scissors, glue and soap
- ● Cork, cardboard and coloured card
- ● Used matchsticks
- ● Aluminium foil, plastic cup
- ● Cotton thread
- ● Red food colouring
- ● Saucepan, long spoon and sieve
- ● Skewer, splint, feather and damp tea towel
- ● Balloon and candle
- ● Paints and paintbrush

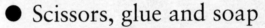

FREEZING

WHAT YOU NEED
*Two plastic drinks bottles
Permanent felt-tip marker
Water
Measuring jug*

WHEN THE WEATHER GETS REALLY COLD, you may have noticed that the water in puddles, ponds and even streams turns solid. This solid water is called ice. As the temperature drops, a chemical reaction takes place which changes the structure of the water. We say that the water freezes, or solidifies, to form ice. Look at some of the differences between liquid water and solid ice in this project.

WHY IT WORKS

Water is made up of tiny molecules which float about at random when the water is liquid. When the water freezes, the molecules join into a box-like framework. This keeps the molecules at a greater distance from each other. As a result, water expands when it freezes and occupies a greater volume.

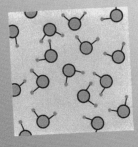

WATER

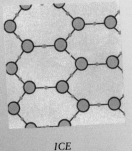

ICE

ICED WATER

Put an ice cube in a glass of water. Ice is made up of molecules which are more spaced out than the molecules in the liquid water. The solid ice is less dense than the liquid water, and weighs less than the same volume of water. As a result, the ice floats on top of the water.

FEELING THE CHILL

1 Use a measuring jug to pour exactly the same amount of water into each of the plastic bottles.

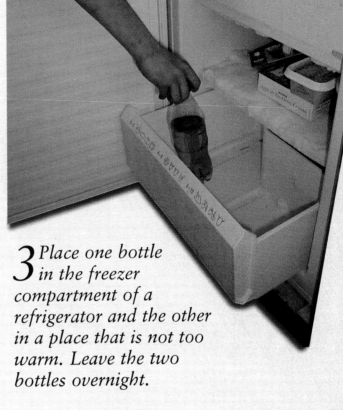

2 Mark the level of the water on the side of each bottle with a permanent felt-tip marker.

3 Place one bottle in the freezer compartment of a refrigerator and the other in a place that is not too warm. Leave the two bottles overnight.

4 Take the bottle from the refrigerator and compare the levels of both bottles. You will see that the level in the bottle containing the ice is higher than in the bottle containing the liquid water.

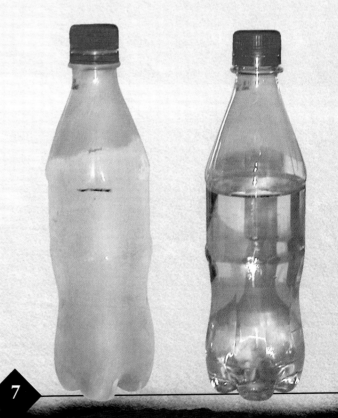

DISSOLVING

WHAT YOU NEED
Three drinking glasses
Water
Measuring jug
Salt
Soil
Fine sand
Plastic cup

IN THE LAST PROJECT, you looked at some of the differences between liquid and solid water. Liquid and solid are known as different states of water. One difference between the two states is that liquid water can absorb and hold certain substances within its structure, but solid ice cannot. This is a chemical reaction called dissolving. However, water cannot absorb every substance, as this project will show.

ONE SUGAR OR TWO?

Look around your home and see if you can find examples where water dissolves other substances. Ask an adult to pour hot water on sugar or coffee granules and see what happens.

NOW YOU SEE IT...

1 *Use a measuring jug to pour the same amount of water into each of the drinking glasses.*

2 *Add some salt to one of the glasses.*

3 *Use a plastic cup to pour some soil into the second glass.*

4 Pour some fine sand into the third glass.

5 Stir all three glasses and leave them for a few minutes.

6 Compare the three glasses. You will see that the salt has disappeared. Most of the soil lies on the bottom of the glass. The water with sand in it is cloudy with a layer of sand at the bottom.

WHY IT WORKS

Salt grains fall apart until they are so small that they can move unseen among the water molecules. They have dissolved. Sand and soil are both made up of small and large particles. Most of the soil particles are too big to dissolve, and they sink to the bottom. The fine particles of sand are small enough to be carried in the water in a cloudy mixture called a suspension.

SALT

SOIL

SAND

SEPARATING SUBSTANCES

WHAT YOU NEED
Drinking glasses
Soil
Water
Sieve
Filter paper
Measuring jug

SOME SUBSTANCES DISSOLVE IN WATER better than others, as you saw in the last project. But how easy is it to separate different substances from the water again? The project on this page will show you how to filter a mixture of soil and water. This will separate the mixture to give you what you started with: soil particles and clear water.

WHY IT WORKS

The holes in the sieve are small enough to stop some soil particles passing through, leaving the mixture a little clearer. The holes in the filter paper are even smaller and only let the tiniest particles pass through with the water. As a result, the mixture is very clear after passing through the filter paper several times.

FILTERING

1 Pour water into a measuring jug and stir in some soil.

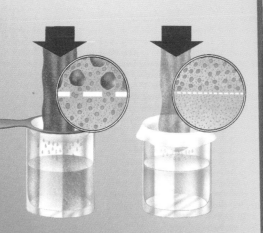

SOIL BLOCKAGE

Repeat the project without the sieve. You may find that the large particles block the holes so that no water can pass through.

2 Place the sieve over a glass and pour through the soil and water mixture. You will see that the water appears slightly clearer, while the sieve now contains particles of soil.

3 Make a cone out of filter paper. Place it over another glass. Pour through what is left of the mixture from the first glass. It will become even clearer and you will see tiny soil particles left on the filter paper.

4 Repeat with clean filter paper and a clean glass. Be careful not to remove the filter paper too soon, as the mixture may take its time passing through.

5 Repeat the filtering until the water running into the glass is clear. You have now separated the soil from the water.

11

BOILING APART

WHAT YOU NEED
Drinking glass
Water
Salt
Saucepan

THE LAST PROJECT SHOWED YOU how to separate soil from water. However, not all substances are as easy to separate from each other. To separate dissolved substances, called solutions, more complicated methods are needed. These methods often make use of differences between the two substances. This project shows you how to separate a solution of salt and water by adding heat.

BRINGING TO THE BOIL

1 *Dissolve the salt in the water in a drinking glass.*

2 *Pour the solution into a saucepan. Ask an adult to boil the solution on a stove. It is very important that you ask an adult to do this for you.*

3 *When all the water has boiled away, ask an adult to turn off the stove and put the saucepan to one side to cool.*

WHY IT WORKS

As the solution is heated, the tiny molecules in it shake rapidly as the heat gives them more and more energy. The water molecules eventually have enough energy to be able to fly off as a gas called steam. This is called boiling. However, the heat does not supply enough energy for the salt molecules to boil, and they are left behind.

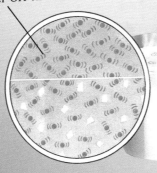

WATER MOLECULES
FLY OFF AS STEAM

4 Look into the saucepan and you will see a layer of white salt. Do not touch it, as it will still be hot.

SUNNY SAUCER

Leave the solution in a saucer on a sunny window ledge. The water will disappear, leaving the salt behind. This works in the same way as boiling the solution, but is slower.

SOAP BOAT

WHAT YOU NEED
Cork
Used
matchsticks
Aluminium foil
Large bowl
of water
Soap
Scissors

HAVE YOU EVER NOTICED THAT when you fill a glass of water right to the brim, the water appears to bulge above the rim of the glass? This is because a force called surface tension holds the tiny molecules of water together, forming a type of skin on the surface of the water. You can break this surface tension by dissolving substances in the water. This project shows you an interesting side-effect of this.

SAIL AWAY

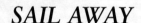

1 *Make a boat by pushing four matchsticks into each side of a cork, as shown. Cut out a small piece of the aluminium foil to make a sail.*

2 *Gently place the boat at one side of the bowl of water. You will find that the boat does not move.*

WALKING ON WATER

Some insects use the surface tension between the water molecules to actually walk on the water's surface. See if you can spot any of these small creatures skimming across the surface of a nearby pond.

3 *Now dab a small piece of the soap onto the back of your boat.*

As the soap dissolves in the water, it breaks up the surface tension between the water molecules behind the boat. This means that the water at the front of the boat then has a greater surface tension which pulls the boat towards it. This causes the boat to move forwards.

SOAP

SURFACE TENSION
OF WATER

SOAP BREAKS SURFACE TENSION

4 Place the boat in the water again at the edge of the bowl. Watch as the boat moves from one side of the bowl to the other.

WORKING WITH PAPER

WHAT YOU NEED
Newspaper
Flour
Water
Balloon
Oil
Paints
Large bowl
Scissors

MANY MATERIALS THAT WE USE every day are made by mixing and separating natural substances. For example, the paper used to make these pages comes from the fibres of trees which have been separated and then squashed together. This project shows you how combining two substances can create a new substance with different properties.

WHY IT WORKS

When you add flour (1) to water, you get a flour and water paste (2). Putting the paper strips into the paste allows the paste to soak into the pores in the paper (3). As the soaked strips dry, the molecules of water float off, or evaporate (4), leaving a hard substance. This is papier-mâché.

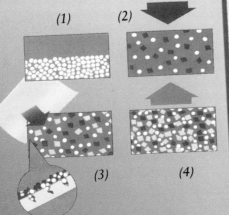

(1) (2) (3) (4)

PAPER MASK

1 Mix the flour and water in a large bowl to form a thick paste. Blow up the balloon and coat it with a thin layer of oil. Tear the newspaper into strips and soak them in the flour and water paste.

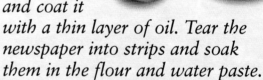

2 Put the soaked strips flat on the balloon. Cover it with about five or six layers of strips. Leave it to dry until the paper has become very hard. This hard substance is called papier-mâché.

3 Ask an adult to carefully cut the papier-mâché from the balloon. The oil should make this a lot easier, but it doesn't matter if the balloon pops. Cut the shape in half to form the mask and then cut out the features.

PAPIER-MÂCHÉ FUN

Think of other objects to make from papier-mâché. You could make a wastepaper bin, using the bin instead of the balloon as your mould.

4 Decorate your mask with paints.

5 If you like, you can turn the hard papier-mâché back into paper and paste. Fill another bowl with water and simply soak the mask in the water.

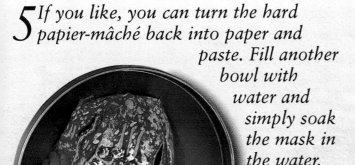

6 The mask becomes floppy when you soak it in water. You have now reversed the papier-mâché-making process.

ADDING HEAT

WHAT YOU NEED
Flour
Water
Large bowl
Skewer
Cotton thread
Paints

SOME FORM OF ENERGY IS OFTEN needed for a chemical reaction to start. The heat in a room may be enough for a substance or mixture to start changing, but in many cases, more heat is needed. For example, china plates and cups have been baked in a very hot oven called a kiln. This turns them from soft clay into hard china. This project shows how heat can turn flour and water into a hard substance.

COOKING JEWELLERY

1 Mix flour and water together in the large bowl to make a dough. Knead the dough well to squeeze out any air bubbles.

3 With the help of an adult, cook the beads in an oven until they have baked hard. Allow them to cool, then push thread through them to form a necklace.

2 Shape and roll the dough into beads like these. Sprinkle flour on your work surface to stop the dough from sticking. Ask an adult to make a small hole in each bead with a skewer. This will let you thread the beads when they are cooked.

MAKING IT EASIER

Change the dough ingredients by adding a little oil. This makes it easier to mould into shape.

4 Decorate the necklace with the paints.

WHY IT WORKS

When flour is mixed with water, it forms a paste or a dough, where the flour molecules are suspended in the liquid. The consistency of the dough depends on how much flour you add. When the dough is baked in the oven, the heat causes the water molecules to evaporate (1), leaving behind a hard substance (2).

(1)

(2)

5 Wear the necklace yourself or give it to someone as a present.

SECRET MESSAGES

WHAT YOU NEED
Lemon
Feather
Sheet of paper
Candle
Jar
Kitchen knife

HEAT PLAYS AN IMPORTANT ROLE in many chemical reactions, not just in turning flour and water into hard clay, as you discovered in the last project. You can see how important heat is every day in any cooked food that you eat. On pages 28-29 you will see how heat is used to make bread. This project shows how heat can turn something that was invisible into something you can see.

INVISIBLE WRITING

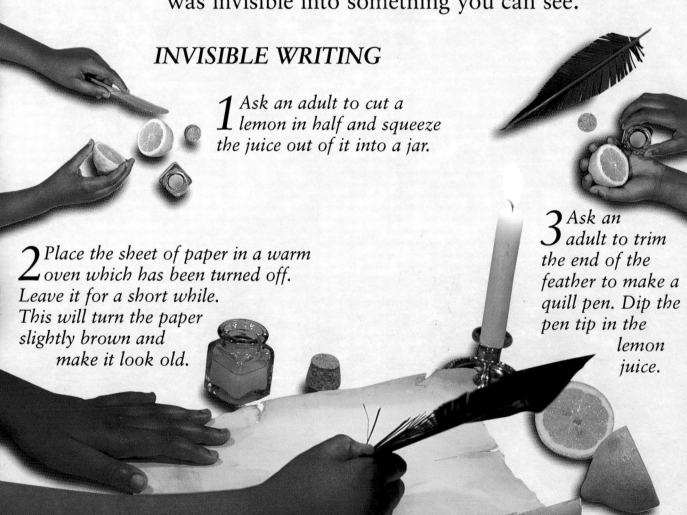

1 *Ask an adult to cut a lemon in half and squeeze the juice out of it into a jar.*

2 *Place the sheet of paper in a warm oven which has been turned off. Leave it for a short while. This will turn the paper slightly brown and make it look old.*

3 *Ask an adult to trim the end of the feather to make a quill pen. Dip the pen tip in the lemon juice.*

4 *Write your secret message on the browned sheet of paper.*

20

MAKING TOFFEE

Ask an adult to help you use heat to make toffee. Mix sugar, water and a drop of vinegar in a saucepan. Bring to the boil, stirring all the time. Remove it from the heat and add bicarbonate of soda. Pour it into a buttered tin. Leave it to cool.

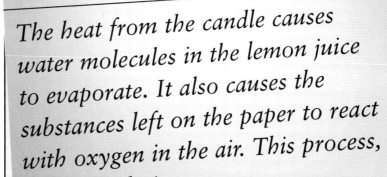

WHY IT WORKS

The heat from the candle causes water molecules in the lemon juice to evaporate. It also causes the substances left on the paper to react with oxygen in the air. This process, called oxidation, turns the lemon juice brown, making it visible.

OXIDISED LEMON JUICE

WATER MOLECULES EVAPORATE

5 To read your message, simply hold the paper close to a lit candle. Ask an adult to do this for you. The message will appear on the paper.

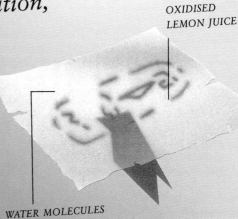

ACIDS AND ALKALIS

ONE WAY OF DESCRIBING CHEMICALS is to say whether they are acids or alkalis. Acids, such as lemon juice, tend to have a sour taste, while alkalis, such as milk, tend to be slightly soapy to the touch. Pure water is neither acid nor alkali – it is described as neutral. Don't try tasting or feeling chemicals at home, though. This project shows you a simpler and safer way to test whether a liquid is an acid or an alkali.

WHAT YOU NEED
Red cabbage
Kitchen knife
Saucepan
Water, Lemon
Blotting paper
Vinegar, Milk
Washing soda
Paintbrush, Jars

FOOD INDICATORS

You can make indicators from other fruits and vegetables. Blackberries and blueberries make good indicators and so does beetroot. Use these to test other liquids around the house.

DETECTING ACIDS

1 *Ask an adult to cut the cabbage into small pieces. Put it in a saucepan and cover it with water.*

2 *Ask an adult to heat the saucepan on the stove. Boil the water and leave it to simmer for 10 minutes. Remove it from the heat and leave it to stand for one hour.*

3 *Strain off the cabbage juice. Dip the blotting paper into it and leave it to dry. This will be your indicator paper.*

4 *Squeeze the juice from a lemon. Pour it, the milk, the vinegar and the washing soda into separate jars.*

22

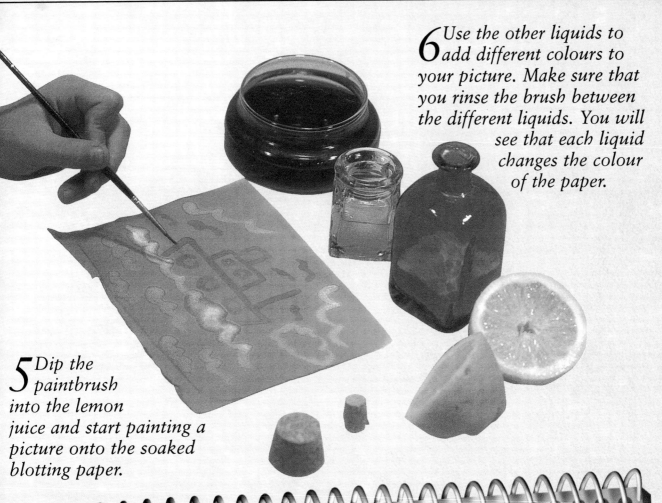

6 Use the other liquids to add different colours to your picture. Make sure that you rinse the brush between the different liquids. You will see that each liquid changes the colour of the paper.

5 Dip the paintbrush into the lemon juice and start painting a picture onto the soaked blotting paper.

WHY IT WORKS

The juice from the cabbage is a good indicator of how acidic or alkaline a substance is. It reacts with the liquid and changes colour according to whether the liquid is acid or alkali. If the liquid is an acid, then the paper will turn red or pink. If the liquid is an alkali, then the paper will turn blue or green.

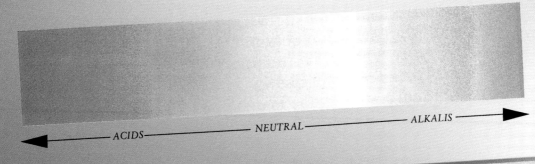

← ─── ACIDS ─── NEUTRAL ─── ALKALIS ──→

BUBBLING VOLCANO

WHAT YOU NEED
Coloured card
Plastic cup
Glue, Water
Newspaper
Paint
Baking powder
Vinegar
Red food
colouring
Cardboard

IN THE LAST PROJECT, you looked at differences between acids such as vinegar and alkalis such as milk. But what would happen if you were to mix acids and alkalis together? Farmers do this regularly, by adding alkali lime to acidic soil to make the soil neutral. This project shows what happens when you mix acidic vinegar with alkaline baking powder – the effects are spectacular.

CHEMICAL VOLCANO

1 *Make a cone by wrapping card around a plastic cup. Glue this firmly to a cardboard base.*

WHY IT WORKS

When the acidic vinegar and the alkaline baking powder mix, they cause a reaction which releases bubbles of a gas called carbon dioxide. These bubbles of gas cause the mixture to froth up and erupt out of your volcano.

2 *Cut off the top of the cone, then glue newspaper strips onto it. Glue on five or six layers of strips. When the strips are dry, paint your volcano and leave it to dry.*

CARBON DIOXIDE

VINEGAR   BAKING POWDER

3 *Mix three parts of water with one part of glue and paint the volcano with the mixture. This will protect the cone when the volcano erupts. Leave this to dry.*

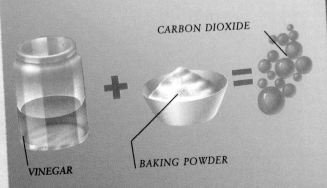

4 Mix some red food colouring with vinegar. Put a teaspoon of baking powder into the volcano.

5 Now pour in the vinegar and food colouring mixture.

FIZZY LEMONADE

Bubbles of carbon dioxide are what make fizzy drinks fizzy. To make fizzy lemonade, mix the juice of four lemons with water and some sugar. Stir in a little bicarbonate of soda. Watch it fizz and then drink it!

6 Watch as red foam erupts out of the volcano, like red-hot lava from a real volcano. The more chemicals you use, the bigger the eruption will be.

GIVING OFF GAS

WHAT YOU NEED
Cork
Used matchsticks
Small candle
Tall jar
Long spoon
Splint
Baking powder
Vinegar
Water

WHEN A FIRE BURNS, a chemical reaction takes place between the burning substance and a gas in the air called oxygen. If there were no oxygen, then the fire could not burn. To put out a fire, firefighters spray water, foam or even carbon dioxide gas to prevent more oxygen from reaching the fire. This project shows how carbon dioxide can extinguish (put out) a lit candle.

FIRE EXTINGUISHER

1 *Make a small boat using the cork and used matchsticks, as shown on pages 14-15. Stick on the candle instead of the mast and sail. Float your boat in some water at the bottom of a tall jar. Ask an adult to light the candle using a splint.*

DIFFERENT SHAPES

See what different kinds of fire extinguisher you can find. Never touch a fire extinguisher as you are looking at it, as it might go off.

2 *Carefully add several spoons of baking powder to the water. Stir the mixture gently with a long spoon.*

3 Quickly pour some of the vinegar into the jar, making sure that you don't spill any onto the lit candle. The liquid should begin to fizz. If it does not, add more baking powder and vinegar.

4 Watch as the liquids at the bottom of the jar fizz and bubble. The candle will dim and finally go out.

WHY IT WORKS

Mixing the vinegar and baking powder together creates bubbles of carbon dioxide. As these bubbles rise from the liquid, they push out the air that was in the jar. Without oxygen in the air, the candle can no longer burn, so it goes out.

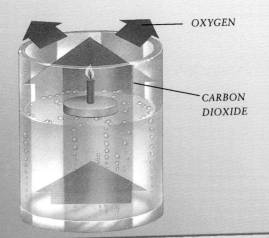

OXYGEN

CARBON DIOXIDE

MAKING BREAD

WHAT YOU NEED
Dried yeast
Caster sugar
Warm water
Wholemeal flour
Butter, Oil
Salt
Large bowl
Clingfilm
Baking tray
Damp tea towel
Board

ALL OF THE REACTIONS YOU HAVE SEEN involve non-living chemicals. These are called inorganic reactions. There are other types of chemical reactions involving living organisms. These are called organic reactions. This project shows you how bread is made and how the chemical reactions of a tiny mould called yeast make bread dough rise.

GETTING A RISE

1 Mix two tablespoons of dried yeast with one teaspoon of sugar and a cup of warm (not hot) water. Leave this mixture until it starts to froth.

2 Mix 500g of flour, two tablespoons of caster sugar, two teaspoons of salt and 25g of butter in a large bowl. Add the yeast mixture and stir in some warm water to form the dough.

3 Place the dough mixture on a floured board and knead it for a while.

WHY IT WORKS

The yeast mould contains special chemicals called enzymes. These react with the sugar to release bubbles of carbon dioxide. The warm water speeds up this reaction. The bubbles of gas cause the bread to rise and take shape.

BUBBLES OF CARBON DIOXIDE

BREAD RISES

4 Rinse, dry and lightly oil the bowl and place the dough in it. Cover the bowl with clingfilm and leave it in a warm place for a few hours.

5 During this time, the dough will rise. When it has finished rising, take the dough out of the bowl and knead it again until it becomes firm. Mould the dough into loaf shapes.

6 Place the dough loaves on a lightly oiled baking tray, brush them with salty water, sprinkle with a little flour and cover with clingfilm. Leave them to rise again.

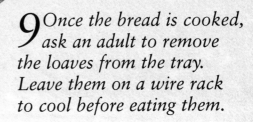

7 Ask an adult to preheat an oven to 220°C (450°F). Remove the dough loaves from the clingfilm and ask an adult to place them and the baking tray in the oven for 30 or 40 minutes.

8 To check if each loaf is cooked, ask an adult to use a damp tea towel to lift it from the tray and tap the base. If it sounds hollow, then the bread is ready. If not, leave it in the oven a little longer.

9 Once the bread is cooked, ask an adult to remove the loaves from the tray. Leave them on a wire rack to cool before eating them.

UNLEAVENED BREAD

Try making the bread without adding the yeast mixture. You will see that the dough does not rise, and you will be left with what is known as unleavened bread.

29

FINDING OUT MORE

ACID This is a type of substance which usually has a sour taste. Vinegar, lemon juice and cola are all acids. *Make your own acid-detecting fluid on pages 22-23 and find out which substances are acidic.*

ALKALI This is a type of substance which is usually soapy to the touch. Baking powder and milk are both alkalis. *The project on pages 22-23 shows you how to detect alkalis.*

BOILING Boiling occurs when the temperature rises and a substance changes its state from a liquid to a gas. *Find out how boiling can separate salt and water in the project on pages 12-13.*

DISSOLVING

Dissolving happens when two substances, such as salt and water, combine completely. When one substance dissolves in another, the result is called a solution.

ACID RAIN

Pollution in the atmosphere around Earth, caused by fumes from industry and cars, has made some rainwater so acidic that it can damage buildings and statues over time.

Look at how some substances can dissolve in water while others can't in the project on pages 8-9.

SUSPENDED SOIL

Rivers carry so much soil in suspension that when they reach the sea and drop the soil particles, areas of land called deltas form.

ICEBERGS

Icebergs are huge chunks of ice that break off the polar ice sheets and float in the sea. Up to four-fifths of each iceberg actually lies below the water line.

SOLUTION

This is a fluid where one substance has dissolved completely in another one. *The project on pages 12-13 shows how to separate a solution of salt and water.*

FREEZING

Freezing is when a substance changes its state from a liquid to a solid as the temperature drops. *Look at freezing in action in the project on pages 6-7.*

ORGANIC

A reaction is organic when it involves living organisms. *The project on pages 28-29 shows you how living organisms help you to make bread.*

SUSPENSION

A suspension is when the particles of one substance float inside another fluid substance. *The project on pages 8-9 shows how fine sand particles float in water in a suspension.*

ANCIENT BREAD

The earliest makers of bread were the Ancient Egyptians. They were producing bread over 5,000 years ago.

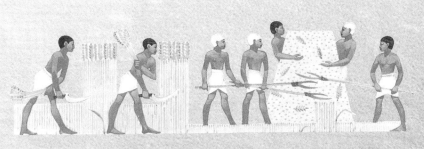

INDEX